VOLCANO!

Ellen J. Prager

ILLUSTRATED BY Nancy Woodman

▢ NATIONAL GEOGRAPHIC SOCIETY

Washington, D.C.

VOLCANO VULCAN

Dragon Explorer

The rocky ground shakes and bulges upward. Then a powerful blast throws rock bombs, gas, and ash high into the sky. Fiery red lava pours from the Earth, and nearby fields of snow and ice melt, creating huge rivers of thick mud.

VOLCANO!

Some volcanoes lie quiet, asleep for many years.

When a volcano sleeps,
beneath its rocky cover all is still and quiet.

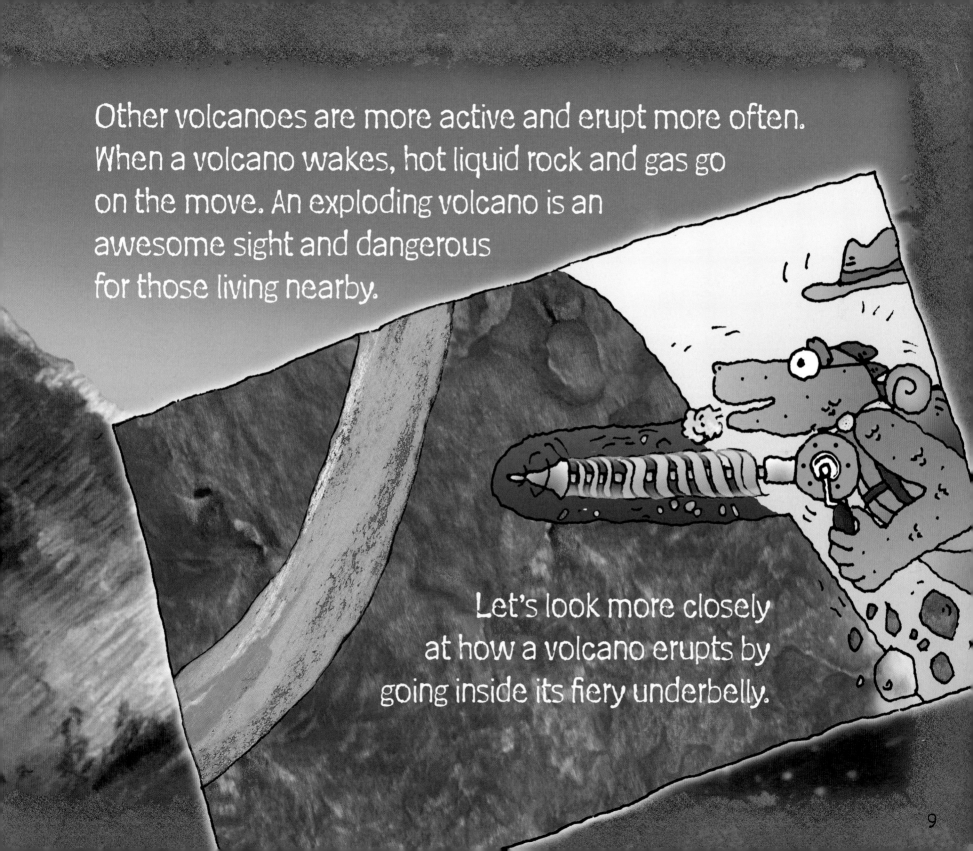

Other volcanoes are more active and erupt more often. When a volcano wakes, hot liquid rock and gas go on the move. An exploding volcano is an awesome sight and dangerous for those living nearby.

Let's look more closely at how a volcano erupts by going inside its fiery underbelly.

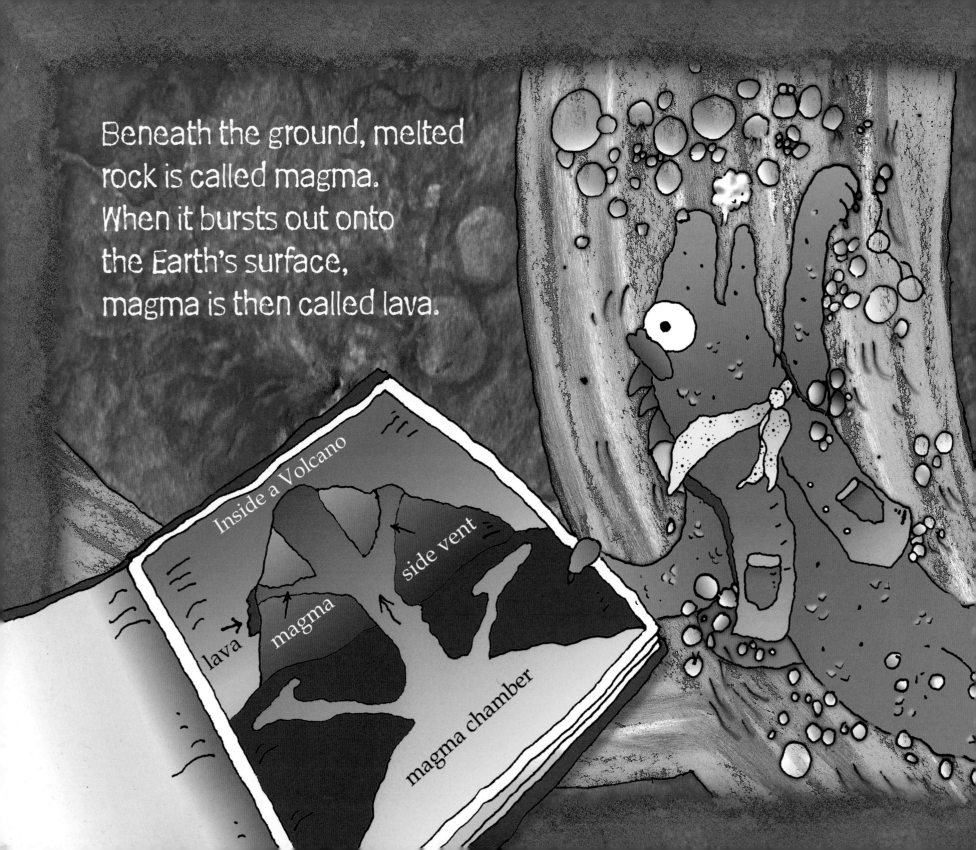

Beneath the ground, melted
rock is called magma.
When it bursts out onto
the Earth's surface,
magma is then called lava.

Inside a Volcano

side vent

lava

magma

magma chamber

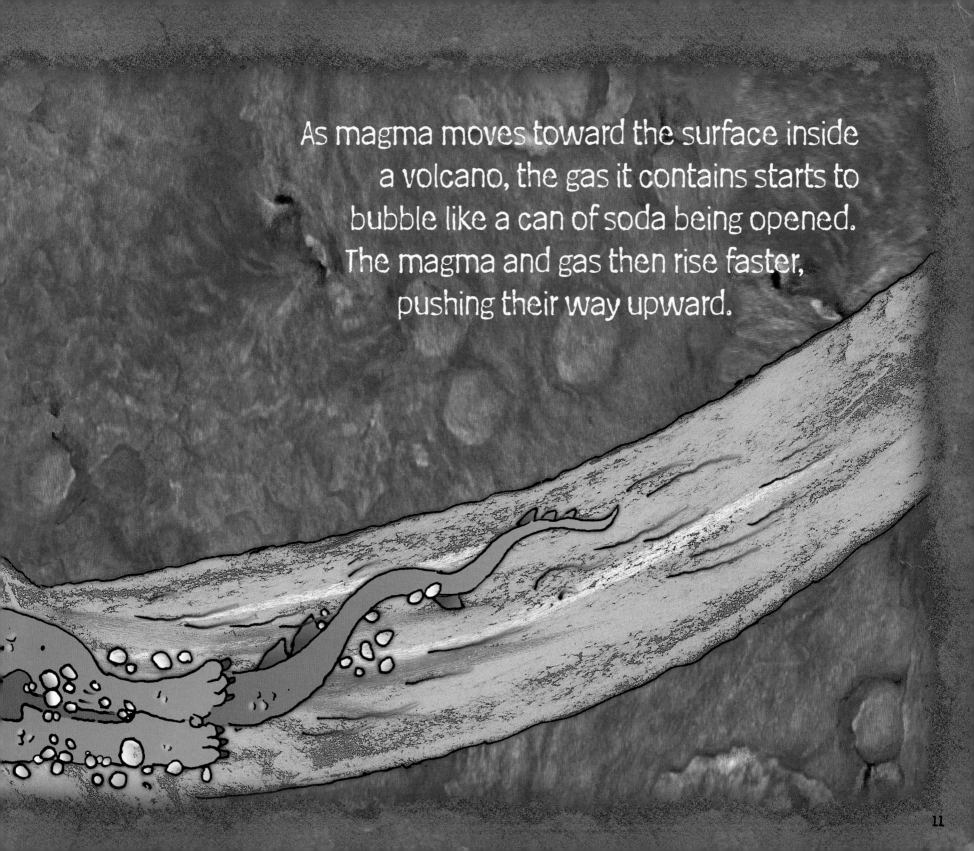

As magma moves toward the surface inside a volcano, the gas it contains starts to bubble like a can of soda being opened. The magma and gas then rise faster, pushing their way upward.

When magma begins to move upward beneath a volcano, the land rumbles and shakes. Earthquakes are often a sign that a volcano is active.

As gas and magma collect
below a volcano's rocky top, the
surface may begin to bulge outward.
Tall pillars of steam shoot skyward as
gas escapes through cracks and holes in the rock.

If too much magma and gas build up, or if an earthquake or landslide pops the volcano's top, it erupts.

VOLCANO!

Often the first sign of an eruption is a huge towering cloud of gas and ash.

Thick clouds of ash block out the sun and turn daylight into darkness. Wind high above a volcano can spread the erupting gas and ash far away. And like a heavy gray snow, the ash falls to the ground and buries all below.

Along with gas and ash, sometimes big rock blocks, or bombs, are thrown out of a volcano's rumbling mouth. Glowing red blobs of lava may also be tossed high into the sky and fall to the ground, forming a giant black cinder cone.

Mud on the Move

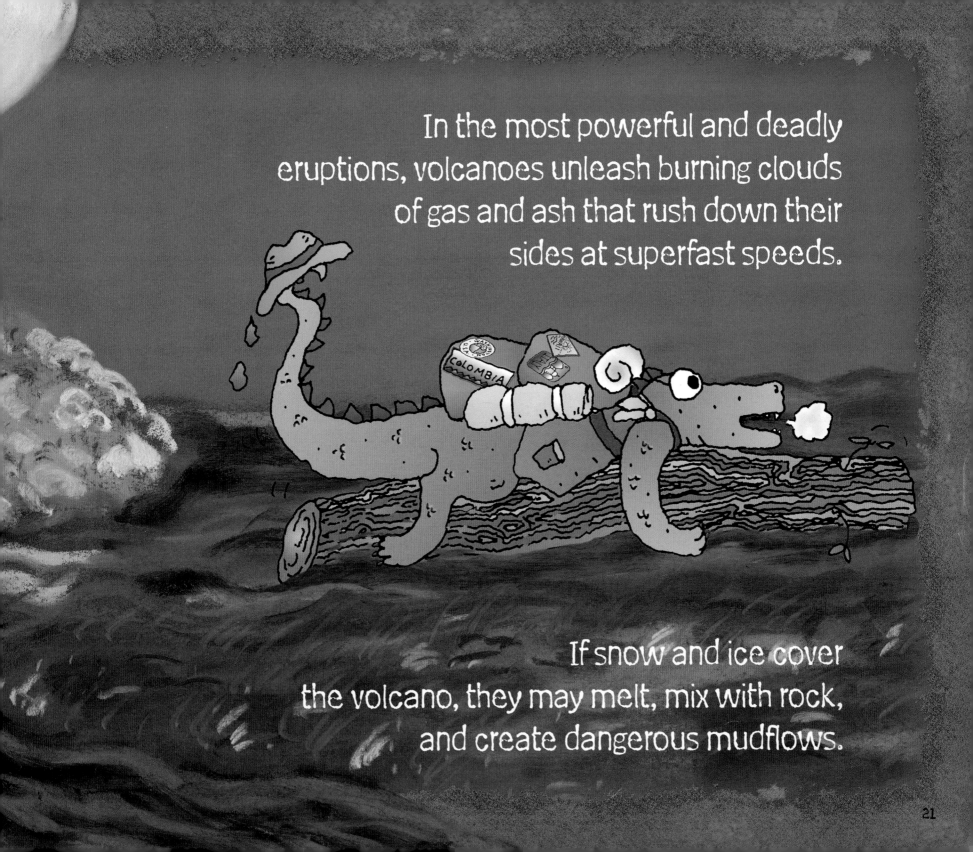

In the most powerful and deadly
eruptions, volcanoes unleash burning clouds
of gas and ash that rush down their
sides at superfast speeds.

If snow and ice cover
the volcano, they may melt, mix with rock,
and create dangerous mudflows.

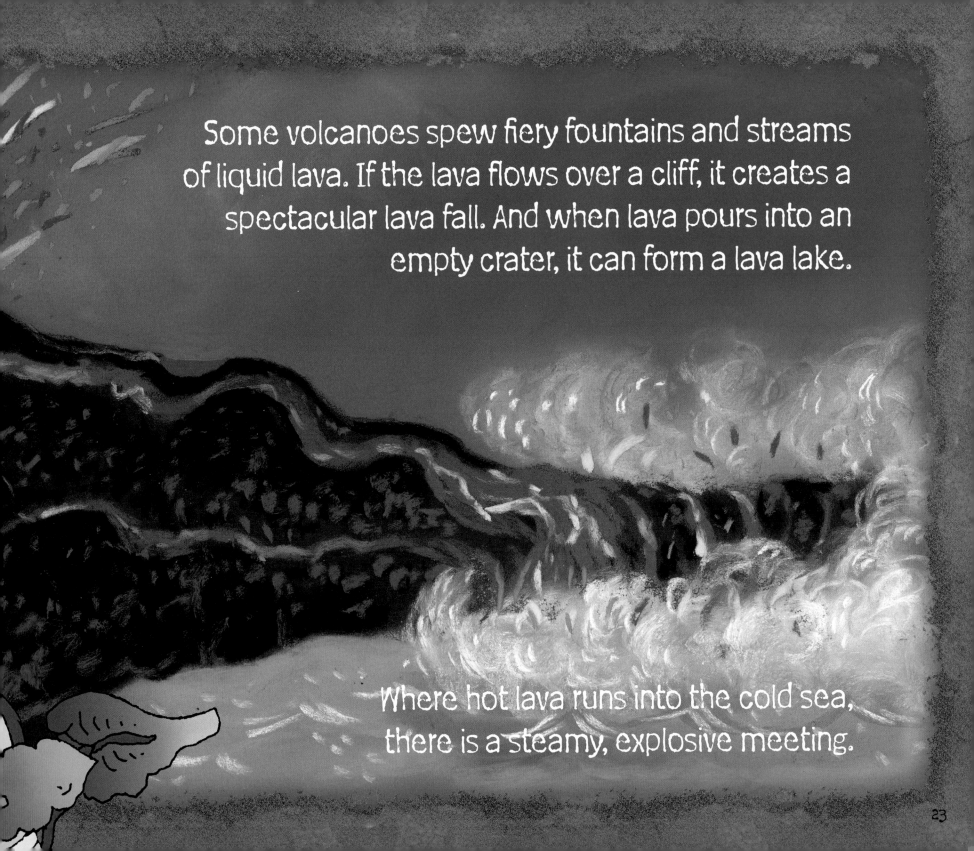

Some volcanoes spew fiery fountains and streams of liquid lava. If the lava flows over a cliff, it creates a spectacular lava fall. And when lava pours into an empty crater, it can form a lava lake.

Where hot lava runs into the cold sea, there is a steamy, explosive meeting.

When lava cools, it hardens into rock. In different places there are different kinds of lava rock depending on what the lava is made of and how it erupted.

In Hawaii there are two types of black lava rock. "Aa" (ahh-ahh) lava is rough and blocky, with very sharp edges. "Pahoehoe" (pah-hoy-hoy) lava looks smooth, like flowing, twisty ropes hardened into stone.

Lava Rock

Aa

Pahoehoe

Scientists study volcanoes all over the world. They want to predict how and when volcanoes will erupt and to warn people living nearby.

Mount Redoubt

Mount Mageik

Mount St. Helens

Iceland

Hawaii

Soufriere Hills Volcano

Nevado del Ruiz

NORTH AMERICA

SOUTH AMERICA

ATLANTIC OCEAN

PACIFIC OCEAN

VOLCANOES OF THE WORLD

= VOLCANIC AREA

Mt. Redoubt, Alaska

Mt. St. Helens, Washington

Soufriere Hills Volcano, Montserrat

Lava blast, Hawaii

Nevado del Ruiz, Colombia

Cinder cone, Iceland

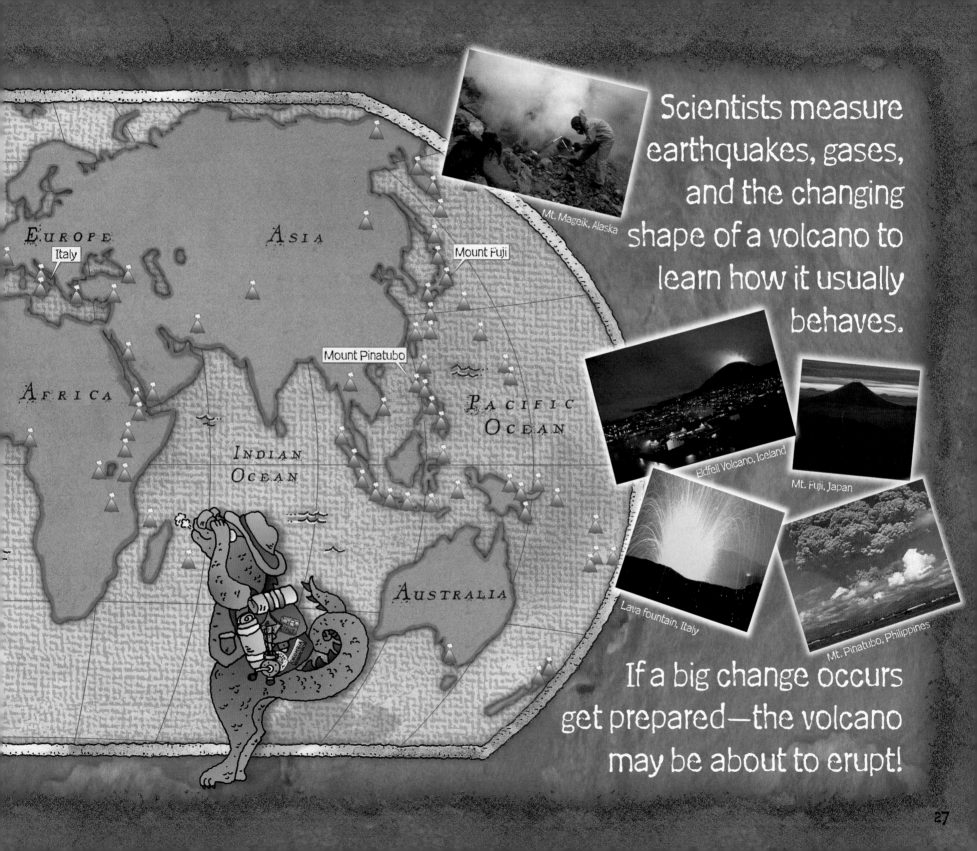

Scientists measure earthquakes, gases, and the changing shape of a volcano to learn how it usually behaves.

If a big change occurs get prepared—the volcano may be about to erupt!

Mt. Mageik, Alaska

Eldfell Volcano, Iceland

Mt. Fuji, Japan

Lava fountain, Italy

Mt. Pinatubo, Philippines

EUROPE
Italy
ASIA
Mount Fuji
AFRICA
Mount Pinatubo
PACIFIC OCEAN
INDIAN OCEAN
AUSTRALIA

Is there a VOLCANO sleeping near you?

28

Build your own VOLCANO!

Here's what you'll need:

- Newspaper
- A drinking straw
- A scoop
- Several cups of flour

1. Make a volcano-shaped mound of flour on the newspaper.

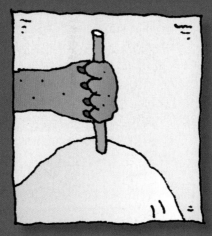

2. Use the straw to make a hole in the top of the volcano.

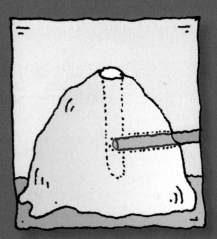

3. Clean out the straw. Stick it through the side of the volcano and into the center.

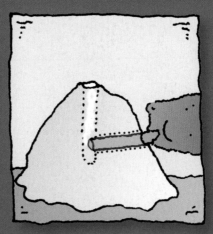

4. Blow very gently into the straw. Then blow a little harder.

Just as in a real volcano, the height of the ash (dry flour) depended on the amount of force from below (you blowing), and where it went, on the flow of air (wind) over the volcano.

Use a mirror to read.

Just as volcano

The flour you blew is like an ash cloud.
What determines the height and direction of the ash?

DR. ELLEN J. PRAGER writes on geology and marine-related topics for children and adults. She's the author of *Sand,* a Parent's Choice winner for 2001, and *Earthquakes.* She lives in Arlington, Virginia, and has observed volcanoes all over the world.

NANCY WOODMAN witnessed the eruption of Mount St. Helens from the beach near her studio. She has been fascinated with volcanoes ever since. She is the illustrator of two other *Jump Into Science* books *Sand* and *Dirt.* She lives in Poulsbo, Washington, and welcomes e-mail at nanneroo@aol.com.

Text copyright © 2001 Ellen J. Prager
Illustrations copyright © 2001 Nancy Woodman

First paperback printing 2007 ISBN: 978-1-4263-0091-2
Published by the National Geographic Society. All rights reserved.
Reproduction of the whole or any part of the contents without written permission from the publisher is prohibited.

The artwork in this book is a digital collage of pastels on sandpaper and pastel paper, watercolors, and photographs.
The type for the book is set in Coventry.
Book design and character concept by Nancy Woodman

Jump Into Science Series Consultant:
Gary Brockman, Early Education Science Specialist

Printed in the United States of America

14/WOR/4

Library of Congress Cataloging-in-Publication Data
Prager, Ellen J.
Volcano! / by Ellen J. Prager; illustrated by Nancy Woodman.
p. cm.
ISBN 0-7922-8201-9
1. Volcanoes—Juvenile literature. [1. Volcanoes.] I. Woodman, Nancy, ill.
II Title.
QE521.3.P73   2001
551.21—dc21   00-011928

PHOTOGRAPHY CREDITS: p. 2 Michael Quearry. p.4 AP/Wide World Photo. p. 16 Michael P. Doukas, USGS. p. 20 left Daniel Dzurisin, USGS; right Lyn Topinka, USGS. p. 22 left David Gaddis; right USGS. p.25 left Robert Dashiell; right David Gaddis. pp. 24-25 lava beach detail based on photo by Fred Hirschmann. p.26 (counterclockwise from top): USGS photo; Jim Valance, USGS; Vincent J. Musi (NGS); Norm Banks, USGS; Robert Patton (NGS); Robert Madden (NGS). p.27 (counterclockwise from top): Bea Ritchie, USGS; Robert Patton (NGS); B. Chouet/USGS; Rick Hobbitt, USGS; George F. Mobley (NGS)

One of the world's largest nonprofit scientific and educational organizations, the National Geographic Society was founded in 1888 "For the increase and diffusion of geographic knowledge." Fulfilling this mission, the Society educates and inspires millions every day through its magazines, books, television programs, videos, maps and atlases, research grants, the National Geographic Bee, teacher workshops, and innovative classroom materials. The Society is supported through membership dues, charitable gifts, and income from the sale of its educational products. This support is vital to National Geographic's mission to increase global understanding and promote conservation of our planet through exploration, research, and education. For more information, please call 1-800-NGS LINE (647-5463) or write to the following address:

NATIONAL GEOGRAPHIC SOCIETY
1145 17th Street N.W.
Washington, D.C. 20036-4688 U.S.A.

Visit the Society's Web site: www.nationalgeographic.com